The Way of
the Cross

Juliette Levivier

Illustrations by Anne Gravier

CTS Children's Books

Table of Contents

Holy week

Jesus went to Jerusalem to celebrate the Passover, as he did every year. This year though, when he entered the city with his disciples, a large crowd came out to meet him shouting, 'Hosannah! Blessed is he who comes in the name of the Lord!'

IT IS PALM SUNDAY

A few days later, while he was sharing his last meal with his disciples, Jesus took the bread and said to them, 'Take this and eat it. This is my body'. Then he took the cup and said to them, 'Take this all of you and drink from it. This is my blood shed for all so that sins may be forgiven.'

This is how he told them that he was going to give his life to save all men.

IT IS MAUNDY THURSDAY

A little later, during the night, Jesus was arrested while he was praying in the Garden of Gethsemene. He was brought before the court and condemned to death.

Then he was whipped and insulted. They mocked him, putting a crown made of thorns on his head and dressing him in a king's cloak.

Then he was led to a hill, not far from the city, to be crucified. At three o'clock in the afternoon, Jesus died on the cross.

After his death, his friends placed his body in a tomb.

IT IS GOOD FRIDAY

Jesus was dead. Everything was over.

Jesus, who brought the love and peace of God his father to all, Jesus who had never committed any sins, had been put to death as a criminal.

So all those who loved him and who believed in him were immensely sad. They felt abandoned and lost.

IT IS HOLY SATURDAY

Very early the next morning, some women, and then some disciples, went to the tomb. It was empty!

Jesus was not there anymore. He is risen from the dead!

Love has overcome violence and death.

IT IS EASTER MORNING

Where the way of the Cross comes from

It was in Jerusalem that Jesus suffered his passion and died on the cross, giving his life for us to save us from sin.

It was there too, three days later, that he rose from death.

A short time later, the first Christians started to go on pilgrimage to Jerusalem to pray at the place where Jesus died and rose to life. They followed the same way that Jesus had walked as he went to the cross.

When they returned home, they wanted to remember this 'way' and to continue to meditate on Jesus' passion.

In the 14th century some Franciscan monks decided to recreate this 'way of the passion' inside churches, for all the people who couldn't go to Jerusalem.

That's why, today, there is a way of the Cross in every church.

In the hope of
the Resurrection

The way of the Cross has fourteen stages
called 'stations'. Each one is
represented by a picture or a statue
or a simple wooden cross.
Some of the stations are episodes
spoken of in the gospels, others are not but
they come from a very old tradition.

The way of the Cross ends with Jesus being
laid in the tomb.

 It would be very sad to stop
there because it's the hope of the
Resurrection which accompanies us
throughout the way of the Cross.

That's why the fifteenth station
speaks of Easter Morning

Jesus invites you
to follow him

When you follow Jesus on this way you can begin to see how incredible his love for you is.

By your prayer, you join in Jesus' suffering and in the suffering of all.

By your prayer, you thank Jesus. He endured everything for you and for all.

When you pray the way of the Cross, Jesus invites you to change your heart to love as only he can love.

For you!

Maybe you have a nice cross on the wall above your bed.

Each time you go into a church, the first thing you do is make the sign of the cross.

This gesture is a prayer. It reminds you, like the cross in your room, that Jesus died and rose to life so that you can have life.

You pray the way of the Cross on Good Friday, but you can also pray it in your family, for example on the Fridays of Lent.

How to pray the way of the Cross

Sit or kneel down and try to keep still.

Read the title of the station, and then say:

'We adore you, O Christ, and we praise you because, by your cross, you have redeemed the world.'

Read the short scripture passage.

In silence, imagine the scene, the noises, the people, the face of Jesus and those who meet him. You can imagine you're with Mary or that you are one of the people who are with Jesus. What prayer comes into your heart?

You can slowly say the prayer that is under the picture.

Jesus is condemned to death

Pilate … having ordered Jesus to be
scourged, handed him over to be crucified.

Mark 15:15

How beautiful is Jesus' gentleness in the face of those
who want to kill him.

How patient he is. How serene.

He answers calmly, but who believes he is the Son
of God?

They refuse to listen to him; they accuse him
of blasphemy.

But how could he speak badly of God? He is the
Word of God.

When I condemn others, when I judge them,

it's you, Jesus, I am rejecting.

Lord Jesus, you have never condemned anyone.

Teach me to love as you alone know how to love.

2nd STATION

Jesus carries his cross

Carrying his own cross,
Jesus went out to the place of the skull,
or, as it was called in Hebrew, Golgotha.

John 19:17

18

How heavy Jesus' cross is! It wounds his shoulders already injured by the blows.

But Jesus carries it himself. He doesn't run away from suffering. He agrees to carry the weight of our sins along with his cross. He agrees to carry the weight of our sufferings along with his cross.

He agrees to carry the weight of our salvation along with his cross. That's how much he loves us.

O Jesus, you help me carry the weight of the great and small sufferings of my life. I pray to you, Lord, for all those who are struggling under the weight of difficulties, injustice and all sorts of suffering.

Jesus falls for the first time

Come to me, all you who labour and are
overburdened, and I will give you rest.

Matthew 11:28

Jesus is exhausted and the cross is so heavy, he falls
beneath its weight. Humbly he stands up again and
continues on his way.

It is our lies, our pride and our wickedness that make
him fall.

Jesus lifts us up again. He takes our cross as well as
his own. He strengthens us.

We are nothing without him.

O Jesus, give me your strength when I am discouraged
and when everything is difficult. Help me to stand up
again and not stay crushed by my sadness.

Jesus meets his mother, Mary

Simeon said to Mary, 'You see this child: he is destined for the fall and rising of many in Israel … and a sword will pierce your own soul too.'

Luke 2:34-35

22   Mary is at the side of the road. She gives Jesus courage and she accompanies him right to the end. Their eyes meet full of love for each other.
Just by being there, she helps him with the strength of her love.
Poor Mary - her heart is pierced with sorrow but she is still full of hope because she knows he is the Son of God.

Lord Jesus, I pray to you for all the children of the
world who are suffering in their bodies or in their
hearts and who don't have a mother near them to
comfort them. May the Virgin Mary, your mother,
give them her tenderness.

Simon of Cyrene helps Jesus to carry his cross

STATION 5th

They seized on a man, Simon from Cyrene, who was coming in from the country, and made him shoulder the cross and carry it behind Jesus.

Luke 23:26

Simon doesn't have a choice. He is pulled out of the crowd to help Jesus. But he has a good heart and he is touched by Jesus' suffering.

He helps Jesus as much by his compassion as by the strength of his arms.

Like Simon, we can help others to carry their 'cross'. We can soothe their hurts and know when they are upset.

Lord Jesus, do you need me to carry your cross?

Make me see when people around me are upset.

When I help them, I am helping you.

Veronica wipes the face of Jesus

Without beauty, without majesty (we saw him),
no looks to attract our eyes, a thing despised
and rejected by men, a man of sorrows … a man
to make people screen their faces.

Isaiah 53:3

How *beautiful* Veronica's face is. How gently she
wipes Jesus' face. How sweet her expression is.
At this gesture, so full of goodness and compassion,
Jesus stops for a moment. His face, marked with so
many scars and with tiredness, imprints itself on the
cloth as she wipes his forehead.
O Jesus, imprint yourself on my heart so that I can
try to be like you.

Like Veronica who wiped your face, with my love
I can try to comfort those who are suffering. O
Jesus, I pray for the sick, the old, the lonely and the
abandoned, and for all those who are sad whom I
would like to console.

Jesus falls for the second time

Harshly dealt with, he bore it humbly, he never opened his mouth, like a lamb that is led to the slaughter house.

Isaiah 53:7

So many people followed Jesus. Was he jostled by the crowd? The path was rough. Did he stumble over a stone? He falls down exhausted. The crowd murmurs. The soldiers are impatient.
Slowly he gets up again and carries on walking.
Our weaknesses and our bad habits often make us fall.
It's Jesus' strength that lifts us up again.

29

Even if I make good resolutions, I find it hard to keep
them! O Jesus, teach me not to become discouraged
and, when I fall, to accept it humbly. Give me your
patience and your strength.

Jesus meets the women of Jerusalem

8th STATION

Jesus turned to them and said, 'Daughters of Jerusalem, do not weep for me. Weep rather for yourselves and for your children!'

Luke 23:28

Along the road some women are crying and lamenting. When they see Jesus pass, exhausted, in front of them, they are filled with pity. Jesus, forgetting his own suffering, breaks his silence to tell them to look at their own sorrows, to open their hearts and to change their lives.

He invites us too to convert our hearts, our thoughts, our words and our actions.

You know, Lord, how much easier it is for me to see
the faults of others than to see my own!
Teach me to recognise my sins and to follow the
way of forgiveness. Help me to come out of my
selfishness and to open my heart.

Jesus falls for the third time

I tell you most solemnly, unless a wheat grain falls on the ground and dies, it remains a single grain; but if it dies, it yields a rich harvest.

John 12:24

Three times Peter denied Jesus. Three times Jesus gave Peter his blessing.

Three times Jesus falls under the weight of his cross. Three times he stands up again.

His strength fails him, but not his will. What a lesson in courage he teaches us!

Out of love for us, he goes to the end of the journey. Three days later, he rises from death.

In spite of all the times I fall, Lord,
I know you always love me.
Thank you, Jesus, for lifting me up again and giving
me the joy of your forgiveness through the
sacrament of Reconciliation.

Jesus is stripped of his clothes

STATION

When the soldiers had finished crucifying Jesus,
they took his clothing and divided it into four
shares, one for each soldier.

John 19:23

All the people are shouting and jostling him. They
mock him with their looks and insult him with their
words. Their hearts are closed.

Jesus is stripped naked and humiliated. He does not
complain. He does not defend himself.

In spite of their offences and insults, he continues to
love them. His dignity shines through.

Lord, you made us in your image and likeness.
So many people suffer insults, ridicule and outrage.
Jesus, you recognise their dignity because you love
them. Teach me to look at the poor with love.

STATION

Jesus is nailed to the cross

Seeing his mother and the disciple he loved standing near her, Jesus said to his mother, 'Woman, this is your son.' Then to the disciple he said, 'This is your mother.'

John 19:26-27

36

See, Mary is still there near Jesus. She does not abandon him.

See, Jesus' feet are pierced through. Will you give him yours to go and preach the gospel?

See, his hands are destroyed. Will you give him yours to serve your brothers?

See, Jesus' arms are open. Will you let his arms close around you?

Yes, Lord Jesus: I will take Mary as my own mother.
With her, I will stand at the foot of the cross.
With her, I will pray that your love will reach all men.

Jesus dies on the cross

12th

STATION

When they reached the place called the Skull,
they crucified him there … Jesus said,
'Father, forgive them; they do not know what
they are doing.'

Luke 23:33-34

38

Listen to the crowd milling round the foot of the cross.
In spite of the shouting, Jesus speaks to his Father.
Listen to his prayer. He is calling on God's mercy
because he has already forgiven those who are
killing him.
He replies to their brutality with gentleness.
He replies to their hatred with love.
Listen to Jesus' cry at the moment of his death.
It is a cry of suffering, but it is also a cry of love.

Lord Jesus, at the hour of your death your arms
are wide open to welcome us and to offer us your
forgiveness. Teach me, Jesus, to forgive others
as you forgive me.

Jesus is taken down from the cross

STATION

When it was evening, there came a rich man of Arimathaea, called Joseph, who had himself become a disciple of Jesus. The man went to Pilate and asked for the body of Jesus. Pilate therefore ordered it to be handed over.

Matthew 27:57-58

40

The crowd has gone.
Mary is still there with John and some others.
There is Joseph of Arimathaea, a friend of Jesus.
His heart aches but he is full of respect. He takes
Jesus down from the cross and places him in Mary's
arms. She holds him for the last time.
Mary prays as her son has taught her.
She cries, she prays, she loves us.

Mary, when you receive Jesus' body, your pain is
boundless but he leaves you his peace.
Jesus, when I pray it's your peace that lives in me.
I want to live in that peace.

14th STATION

Jesus is laid in the tomb

So Joseph took the body, wrapped it in a clean shroud and put it in his own new tomb … He then rolled a large stone across the entrance of the tomb and went away.

Matthew 27:59-60

Suddenly, there is only silence and emptiness!
Jesus is no longer seen, no longer heard. No one can touch him or speak to him anymore.
Everything seems lost. Everyone has gone back to their homes, back to their old lives.
Mary waits and prays in front of the tomb. It has become the tabernacle where the body of Christ rests.
Through the Eucharist, he comes to renew our hearts.

43

It is in the silence, Jesus, that you reveal yourself.

In the Eucharist, Jesus, you give yourself to me.

When I see the host, it is you I contemplate.

15th STATION

Jesus rises from the dead

The angel spoke, and he said to the women,
'There is no need for you to be afraid. I know
you are looking for Jesus who was crucified. He
is not here, for he has risen as he said he would.'

Matthew 28:5-6

44

It is a beautiful Easter Morning!

Nature is reborn on this spring morning. The rays of
the sun light up the women who are going up to the
tomb. They are amazed! The tomb is empty!

An angel reassures them. They run quickly to tell the
apostles, 'He is alive!'

With Jesus, let's come out of our tombs!

Let's leave our selfishness, our resentment, our
sadness. With him we are called to the Resurrection.

Alleluia!

O Jesus, make me a witness to your love.
May the light of your resurrection light up my heart
and shine through my eyes, breaking through in all
I say and do!

CTS Children's Books

The Beautiful Story of Jesus, *by Maïte Roche* (CTS Code CH 13)

Benedict and Chico, *by Jeanne Perego* (CTS Code CH 12)

The Bible for little children, *by Maïte Roche* (CTS Code CH 2)

First prayers for little children, *by Maïte Roche* (CTS Code CH 5)

Getting to Know God, *by Christine Pedotti* (CTS Code CH 9)

The Gospel for little children, *by Maïte Roche* (CTS Code CH 1)

Max and Benedict, *by Jeanne Perego* (CTS Code CH 24)

The Most Beautiful Christmas Story, *by Maïte Roche* (CTS Code CH 8)

My Little Missal, *by Maïte Roche* (CTS Code CH 20)

Prayers around the Crib, *by Juliette Levivier* (CTS Code CH 7)

Praying at Mass, *by Juliette Levivier* (CTS Code CH 11)

Praying with Mary, *by Juliette Levivier* (CTS Code CH 14)

Praying with the first Christians, *by Juliette Levivier* (CTS Code CH 10)

Praying with the Friends of Jesus, *by Juliette Levivier* (CTS Code CH 6)

Praying with the Holy Spirit, *by Juliette Levivier* (CTS Code CH 15)

The Rosary, *by Juliette Levivier* (CTS Code CH 3)

Saint Anthony of Padua, *by Silvia Vecchini* (CTS Code CH 16)

Saint Francis of Assisi, *by Silvia Vecchini* (CTS Code CH 17)

Saint Lucy, *by Silvia Vecchini* (CTS Code CH 19)

Saint Paul, *by Silvia Vecchini* (CTS Code CH 22)

Saint Rita of Cascia, *by Silvia Vecchini* (CTS Code CH 18)

Saint Thérèse of Lisieux, *by Silvia Vecchini* (CTS Code CH 23)

The Way of the Cross, *by Juliette Levivier* (CTS Code CH 4)

The Way of the Cross: Published 2006 by the Incorporated Catholic Truth Society, 40-46 Hurleyford Road, London SE11 5AY. Tel: 020 7640 0042; Fax: 020 7640 0046; www.cts-online.org.uk. Copyright © 2006 the Incorporated Catholic Truth Society in this English language edition.

ISBN: 978 1 86082 398 5   CTS Code CH 4

Le chemin de croix: (La prière des petits), by Juliette Levivier, illustrations by Anne Gravier, published 2006 by Edifa-Mame, 15-27 rue Moussorgski, 75018 Paris; ISBN Edifa 2-9145-8026-6; ISBN Mame 2-7289-1073-1. Copyright © Groupe Fleurus 2006.